CHURCHILL DOWNS

SHOE WORN BY STREET SENSE IN THE 2007 KENTUCKY DERBY, SHOWN ACTUAL SIZE.

Only a handful of the exuberant crowd at Churchill Downs were sitting as the full field of contenders raced around the first turn against the familiar backdrop of the track's historic Twin Spires in the 133rd running of the $2 million guaranteed Kentucky Derby on May 5, 2007.

Jockey Calvin Borel closed in on his first victory in the Kentucky Derby as he urged James Tafel's Street Sense clear of runner-up Hard Spun on the way to a 2 ¹⁄₄-length victory in the 2007 "Run for the Roses."

KENTUCKY DERBY

133 REVIEW

A Moonlight Press Book

CREDITS

Kentucky Derby: 133 Review

©2007 Moonlight Press. All Rights Reserved.

ISBN 9780970963956
Library of Congress Control Number 2007937017

Executive Editor: Leonard Lusky
Creative Director: Cary Meyer
Administrative Assistants: Kelli Garvey
Copy: John Asher, Churchill Downs, Vice President of Racing
Communications   ---

Contact Information:
Moonlight Press
P.O. Box 4865
Louisville, KY 40204
502.473.1036 Phone
e-mail: derbyreview@secretariat.com

Please contact us for more information regarding orders, volume discounts and corporate customization.

Thanks to Street Sense – a horse so talented that my support on Derby Day couldn't stop him – along with Carl and Wanda Nafzger, Ian and Tracey Wilkes, Calvin Borel and Lisa Funk, Jerry Hissam, Jim Tafel and the entire Street Sense team. Special thanks for inspiration to Col. Matt Winn, Jim Bolus and Mike Barry -- who would have loved everything about Derby 133. My deepest gratitude for faith and friendship to James Ausenbaugh, William McKeen, C.E. Henson, Jr., and Brian Rublein. Love always to Emma, Erin and Heather – the Regret, Genuine Risk and Winning Colors in my life – and to Dolores Asher (#1) and Jennye Beeler (#1A), Eternal thanks to The Book for making every day feel like Kentucky Derby Day.   --- John Asher

Moonlight Press also wishes to thank Cheri Noel, Emily Cotton, Rich Cleaves, Margie Ogawa, and Richard & Leonard Barlow.

End-pages by artist Misha Lenn, courtesy of JettStream Productions.

Photographers:

Chris Burkhardt	Bryon Butler
John Chan	Pam Davis
Larry Foster	Bruce Fratto
Christine George	Phil Groshong
Dave Hooker	Lisa Huber
John Sattler	Ray Schuhmann
Tom Schuhmann	David Toczko
Antz Wettig	Jon Wettig
Al Wollerton	Christine Zalewa
Don Zalewa	

Director of Photography: Ray Schuhmann
Derby Archivist: Ann Tatum
Art Director: Tim Pitts
email: DerbyArchives@Kinetic.Distillery.com
Website: www.DerbyArchives.com

Contact Information:
Kinetic Corporation
200 Distillery Commons, Suite 200
Louisville, KY 40206-1990
502.719.9500 Phone
502.719.9509 Fax

All of the imagery is from the Official Kentucky Derby Photographic Archives. Kinetic has been the Official Photographer and Archivist for the Kentucky Derby for over 50 years.

Individual print orders of any of these images, or any previous years Derby, are available by calling the Kentucky Derby Photo Archivist at 502.719.9500 or placing an order on-line at the above website address. For best rates enter "KD133mp" in the Promotion Code box. Commercial and editorial use also available, permission must be granted.

Opposite Page: 2007 Kentucky Derby winning jockey, Calvin Borel.

In the world of Thoroughbred racing – and perhaps in the realm of American sport – there is no dream that is more grand or alluring than a victory in the Kentucky Derby under the venerable Twin Spires of Churchill Downs.

Every year since 1875, crowds have gathered on a plot of land just south of downtown Louisville, Ky. to watch 3-year-old Thoroughbreds compete in a race that, on the first Saturday in May, becomes much larger than the sport itself and captivates the nation and the racing world. A victory in the Kentucky Derby is the ultimate dream in American racing and breeding. It is a daily goal and obsession for all who make their living in the business, from the most humble groom to the wealthiest of men and women who own the horses that are being directed toward the 1 1/4-mile race at Churchill Downs.

There are no guarantees on the road to the Kentucky Derby. The race can be won by a horse that fetches a high price in the auction ring, as $4 million yearling purchase Fusaichi Pegasus proved when he won the race in 2000. But more often the race is won by a horse whose beginnings are more similar to those of Seattle Slew, a $17,500 yearling purchase who in 1977 would become the first unbeaten winner of the Triple Crown, a three-race sweep that also includes victories in the Preakness at Baltimore's Pimlico Race Course and the Belmont Stakes at New York's Belmont Park. The winner of the 1971 Derby, Canonero II, was grabbed from a yearling sale for a winning bid of only $1,200.

Then there is the partnership that raced 2003 Derby winner Funny Cide – a group of high school buddies from upstate New York known as Sackatoga Stable who entered the racing business on a virtual whim and pooled individual investments of $5,000 to buy their first horse. The partners would eventually purchase Funny Cide for $22,000 at a sale for horses bred in New York and the rest, as it has been said, is Derby history.

There's an adage in racing that "a good horse can come from anywhere," and that notion fuels the intrigue inspired by the famed "Run for the Roses."

The Kentucky Derby and its historic home grew from the inspiration of Col. Meriwether Lewis Clark, who founded The Louisville Jockey Club in 1875. The race course featured a schedule of races headed by the first running of the Kentucky Derby, a 1 1/2 mile event restricted to 3-year-old Thoroughbreds and modeled after the Epsom Derby, Britain's classic race for horses of that age group that was first run at Epsom Downs in 1780. Clark, the grandson of William Clark of the famed Lewis & Clark Expedition, wanted a racetrack in Louisville that could showcase the high quality Thoroughbreds that were already being produced on farms built atop the lush bluegrass and limestone enriched soil of Central Kentucky's horse country.

The Kentucky Derby struggled in its early years, but the arrival in 1902 of a management team led by the legendary Col. Matt Winn, who was first the track's general manager and eventually its president, provided the spark and the momentum that lifted the Kentucky Derby to its now long-held status as America's greatest horse race and one of the world's great sports events.

Under Col. Winn's guidance, and with the help of legendary horses and horsemen who have participated in the race in the decades since, the Kentucky Derby assumed its place in the hierarchy of the most acclaimed sports events in the United States and the world. But one of Winn's greatest accomplishments was to craft a celebration that was as much social spectacle as great sporting event. The Kentucky Derby, run for the 133rd consecutive year in 2007, is an event that is a celebration of Americana and a rite of Spring.

Kentucky-born humorist and author Irvin S. Cobb once struggled to find the adequate words to describe the magic conjured each year when

the call to the post is sounded, the strains of "My Old Kentucky Home" fill the air, and young horses break from the starting gate in a quest for glory that is bestowed on only one horse each year, with just one opportunity to grasp that moment in the spring of their 3-year-old year.

"If I could do that, I'd have a larynx of spun silver and the tongue of an anointed angel," Cobb said.

But he ultimately found the words that are as accurate a description of the lure of the Derby as one could hope to find:

"Until you go to Kentucky and with your own eyes behold the Derby, you ain't never been nowheres and you ain't never seen nothin'!"

— Irvin S. Cobb

15

tradition

Generations of Kentucky Derby fans have gathered annually at Churchill Downs since more than 10,000 people witnessed the first running of the classic for 3-year-old Thoroughbreds on May 17, 1875. America's greatest race has been renewed annually without interruption, making it through

High fashion and mint juleps became essential ingredients in the Kentucky Derby as the race grew rapidly through the early decades of the 1900's to emerge as a spectacular social celebration as well as America's greatest race and one of the world's most popular sports events.

Wars, the Great Depression and a devastating Ohio River flood in 1937 to become a sports icon and America's oldest continuously held sports event.

Brilliantly colored hats of every imaginable color and design are as much a part of Kentucky Derby tradition as the mint julep and the fabled Derby roses, and finding the perfect hat can be as challenging in its own way as picking the right horse on race day.

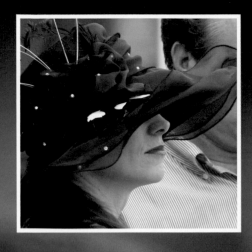

spectacle

Col. Matt J. Winn – the revered architect of the Kentucky Derby and Churchill Downs as we know them today – described his sprawling racetrack as a "monstrous crazy-quilt structure" with a "heart and soul, and a serene personality."

The Colonel's words are not a bad place to start when it comes to describing the allure of the annual rite of spring that is the Kentucky Derby. The day is a wondrous mix of sports event, social gathering, fashion show, frat party, and backyard family

Spanning several generations, the evolution of the Kentucky Derby as a major sporting event has created a soaring demand for prime on-track viewing locations, and this inventive group of fans was no exception as they gathered atop the roof of a Churchill Downs barn to view the 1940 Derby.

picnic. All that activity is compressed into cozy sections of the historic track's grounds.

The "crazy-quilt" collection of more than 150,000 fans who share in the spectacle become one when all action stops for the pre-race serenade of "My Old Kentucky Home," followed with a full-throated communal roar when the Derby field turns for home and flashes past the time-honored Twin Spires.

The compelling cast that provides the character of each Derby extends beyond the equine and human stars on the track. Only on a stroll through the infield could one find inspiring fashion choices, with the duo at left being prepared should they stumble on an infield luau or siesta, or visit with the Queen of England or Kentucky icon Col. Sanders above (or reasonable facsimiles thereof). And as the faces in the crowd can attest, the universal appeal of the Derby guarantees a grand experience that far exceeds the good fortune derived from any winning wager.

While springtime in Kentucky provides an explosion of natural color and excitement, the sensations of the season reach spectacular new heights on Derby Day. Indelible images of Derby133 included flag bearers, left, who formed a perfect line while awaiting the opening notes of "My Old Kentucky Home"; young fans who struck up an equine friendship at the track, right; and artist Peter Williams,below, whose brush deftly-committed the Derby's swirling colors to canvas in the track's Paddock.

ROYALTY

the queen

It took 133 years for a British monarch to visit Churchill Downs, and the presence of Her Majesty Queen Elizabeth II made Derby Day 2007 one of the most special in the track's history. The Queen and her husband, Prince Philip, were accompanied by William S. Farish, the former U.S. Ambassador to England who owns Lane's End Farm in Versailles, Ky. and once served as chairman of the board of Churchill Downs.

"Queen Elizabeth is certainly the most prestigious guest we've entertained in the modern day history of the Kentucky Derby," said Steve Sexton, President of Churchill Downs.

Jerry Abramson, the Mayor of Louisville's Metropolitan government, was among those who welcomed the 81-year-old monarch as she experienced the Kentucky Derby for the first time. "It says something about the Derby that it has universal appeal from the royals to us regular folks," said Abramson.

Her Majesty Queen Elizabeth II and her husband, Prince Philip, the Duke of Edinburgh, paid their first visit to Churchill Downs and joined a crowd of 156,635 to witness the victory by Street Sense.

oaks

While the Kentucky Derby became an American icon in the early decades of the 1900's, it took a while longer for its sister race – the Kentucky Oaks – to hit its best stride. The 1 1/8-mile race for 3-year-old fillies is the traditional centerpiece of a stellar racing program on the eve of the Kentucky Derby, but an era of explosive growth over the last 25 years has placed the Oaks firmly near the top of American racing's most popular attractions.

Like the Kentucky Derby, the Oaks has been run annually without interruption since its introduction. The day of racing that surrounded the Oaks became known as "Louisville's day at the races" in the mid-1900's as local residents, many of whom found it increasingly difficult to secure seating for the Derby, took in a day at the track on Derby Eve.

Rain pelted Churchill Downs on Kentucky Oaks Day, but the wet and dreary weather could not douse the excitement generated by the brilliance of Rags to Riches as she earned the race's traditional garland of lilies with one of the most dominant victories in Oaks history.

RAGS TO RICHES

Before the running of the 133rd Kentucky Derby, there were more than a few racing fans and observers who openly hoped that a chestnut filly named Rags to Riches would bid for the roses.

A daughter of A.P. Indy and a half sister to 2006 Belmont Stakes winner Jazil, Michael Tabor and Derrick Smith's filly instead was pointed by trainer Todd Pletcher toward the Kentucky Oaks. She came into the Derby's sister race with a three-race winning streak and scored an emphatic 4 1/4-length victory under jockey Garrett Gomez. She covered 1 1/8-miles in 1:49.99 and dominated 13 rivals over a "muddy" racing surface under the Twin Spires that she may not have particularly cared for.

"We worried about the weather, she'd never really been behind other horses," said Pletcher. "But she's an unbelievable filly, a true superstar."

Those who had hoped that Rags to Riches would take on the boys in the Kentucky Derby had a chance to smile five weeks later when Tabor and Smith's filly turned back Preakness winner Curlin to become the first filly in a century to win the Belmont Stakes, the final jewel of the Triple Crown.

Jockey Garrett Gomez celebrates his first victory in the 133rd renewal of the Kentucky Oaks aboard the chestnut filly Rags to Riches. Despite the muddy track, her commanding victory marked the sixth-fastest time in the history of the Oaks run at the 1 1/8 mile distance.

But the popularity of the Kentucky Oaks has soared in recent decades. A total of 100,075 fans gathered at Churchill Downs for the 2007 Oaks, marking the seventh time in eight years that attendance at the race had exceeded 100,000. This impressive growth has coincided with the establishment of several traditions distinctive to the race, that include the presentation to the winner of a mantle of Stargazer Lilies, the Oaks counterpart to the Derby's famed roses.

"The Oaks is one of those coveted races that all trainers would like to win," said Hall of Fame trainer D. Wayne Lukas, who has won the race four times. "I think you can go in there to Churchill Downs on Friday and Saturday and if you win either one of them, you can come out of there with a pretty good feeling."

The list of distinctive and poignant moments on any Kentucky Derby Day can be endless, but very much up to the discretion of the individual and his or her particular level of participation. But one part of Derby Day has become increasingly popular in recent years, and it could be argued that it is the most hopeful and romantic moment of a day with a foundation that is, quite basically, the pursuit of dreams.

Call it "The Walk," if a label must be placed on it. The Derby horses pass through a small backstretch gate known as "the gap," and anticipation mounts as they edge closer to America's greatest race. When the call is given, each horse is led clockwise around the track's first turn toward the Paddock, where they will be saddled and final adjustments are made in preparation for the biggest race of their lives.

The Walk is a blur of emotions and sensations. Along with the grooms that lead them, each Derby horse is usually accompanied by team members that can include trainers, owners, family and friends – all dressed in their Derby finery and ready to celebrate. Derby-goers in reserved seats tiptoe to get a good look at their Derby favorite, while infield revelers from all walks of life shout out the names of their chosen horses.

Within an hour, the disappointment of the day will be crushing for those surrounding all but one very special horse. But the dream of winning the Kentucky Derby is never more alive than during the moments that make up "The Walk."

the Walk

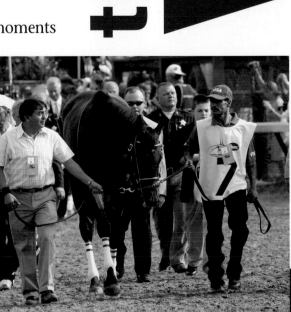

With each step around that first turn, the start of the Derby draws nearer and the Twin Spires loom larger – close enough, it seems, that one could reach out and embrace those century old icons. Out of an American foal crop that numbered just over 37,000 when these horses hit the ground three years earlier, a maximum of 20 Thoroughbreds and the humans behind them get to experience this moment. Leading the parade of Derby hopefuls was James Tafel's Street Sense, right, followed by Imawildandcrazyguy, top, and Any Given Saturday, above.

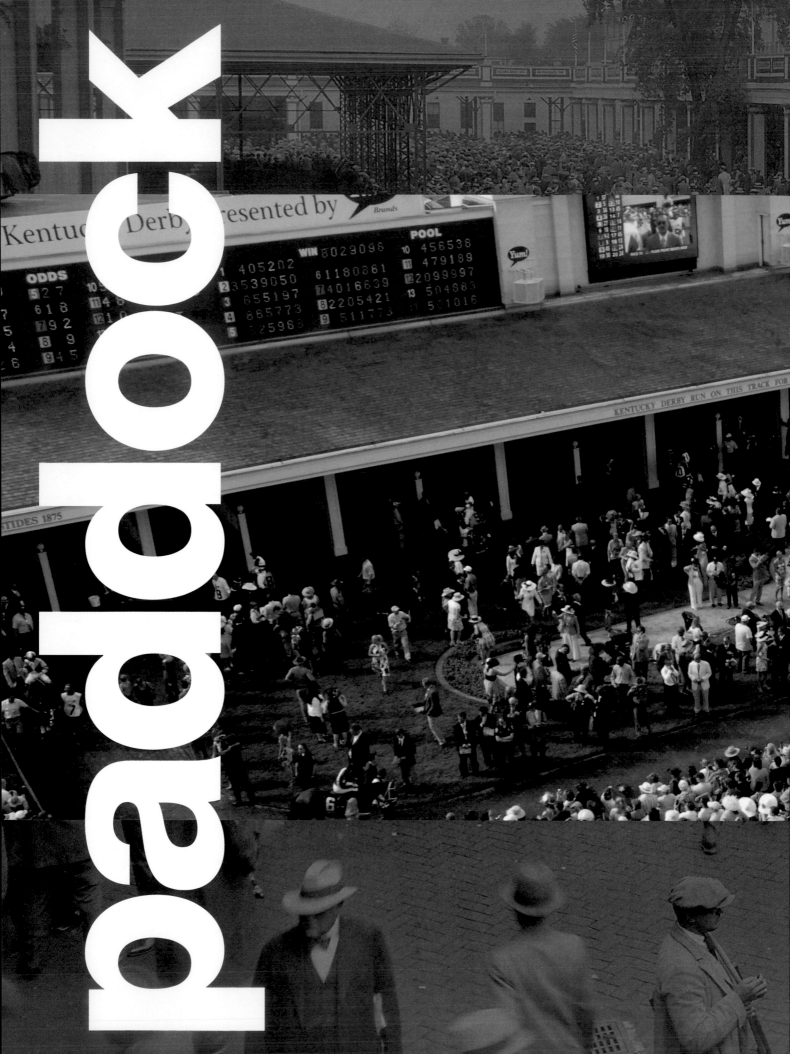

By the standards of the area that existed prior to 1986, the current Paddock is sprawling. But despite the added space, the demand for access to a few inches of that real estate in the form of a Paddock entry pass has soared, which leaves just enough room for horses and humans as the Derby entrants are being saddled. Just across the fence that separates the saddling enclosure from the Paddock Garden, the surging crowd can stack up dozens deep.

THE PADDOCK

The current Paddock at Churchill Downs was first used in 1986, when it replaced a small and claustrophobic structure located adjacent to the current saddling area. That original paddock, which was later enclosed and dubbed The Paddock Pavilion, was the scene of pre-race activity beginning in the 1920's and 10 of the 11 horses that swept racing's Triple Crown were saddled prior to their Kentucky Derby victories in the historic enclosure. For the Centennial Derby in 1974, a record field of 23 horses squeezed into the tiny area for the big event.

Naturally nervous and curious horses are reason for special concern when it comes time to saddle entrants for the Kentucky Derby.

Contenders visit the Paddock for schooling during Derby Week – sometimes making several visits to acclimate to the presence of people inside and outside of the enclosure. How their horse will handle the close quarters and the flood of new sensations on Derby Day is a question for every trainer and owner. The Paddock is yet another hurdle for the horse best prepared to handle both the mental and physical challenges posed by America's greatest race.

Before a festive and noisy crowd, Street Sense with jockey Calvin Borel aboard, was a picture of cool professionalism in the Paddock prior to Derby 133 – the same demeanor he would adroitly display in his stretch-running victory a few minutes later.

The stroll from the Paddock to the track minutes before the running of the 133rd Kentucky Derby foreshadowed the final result as Street Sense and jockey Calvin Borel stepped onto the track just ahead of eventual runner-up Hard Spun and rider Mario Pino.

There was no shortage of talent and experience in the ranks of trainers of horses that participated in the 2007 renewal of the Kentucky Derby, despite the absence from the race of a trio of trainers whose exploits had made them its most dominant forces over the last two decades.

For the first time since 1980, there was no horse in the race trained by multiple Derby winners D. Wayne Lukas (1988, '95, '96 & '99), Bob Baffert (1997, '98 & 2002), or Nick Zito (1991, 1994).

But three Derby-winning trainers were on hand for the event, including Texas-born Carl Nafzger who hoped to become a two-time winner of the "Run for the Roses" with James Tafel's Street Sense. He had previously won with Unbridled in 1990.

The other former Derby-winning trainers who participated in Derby 133 were John Shirreffs (Giacomo, 2005), who would saddle seventh-place finisher Tiago, and Barclay Tagg (Funny Cide, 2003), whose Nobiz Like Shobiz would finish 10th.

Todd Pletcher, the winner of three consecutive Eclipse Awards as America's top trainer, saddled five of the 20 starters in Derby 133 and Circular Quay,

who came in sixth, finished the best of those. His Kentucky Oaks-winning filly Rags to Riches would provide some redemption five weeks later with a memorable Belmont Stakes victory over Curlin, the Derby's third-place finisher and eventual Preakness winner, that gave Pletcher his first win in a Triple Crown event. But the setbacks by his quintet in the 2007 Kentucky Derby left Pletcher still yearning for the scent of roses – and a record 19 Derby entrants without a victory.

parade

There are few moments in American sport that are more sentimental and stirring than the post parade for the Kentucky Derby. After the horses have been saddled in the Paddock, the call of "Riders up!" rings out, and the jockeys are given a leg-up into the irons and the 3-year-olds that have made it to the "Run for the Roses" make their way to the historic one-mile track for their date with history.

As the first horse steps onto the track, bugler Steve Buttleman plays the traditional "Call to the Post," but that familiar collection of musical notes possesses an electricity on the first Saturday in May that could not be recreated on any of the other 364 dates on the year's calendar. Once the horses emerge from the Paddock walkway, they turn and line up behind the track's lead outrider as the University of Louisville marching band plays the opening notes of Stephen Foster's "My Old Kentucky Home."

Julien Leparoux
Sedgefield

Robby Albarado
Curlin

Shaun Bridgmohan
Zanjero

Juan Leyva
Storm in May

Mark Guidry
Imawildandcrazyguy

Fernando Jara
Cowtown Cat

Calvin Borel
Street Sense

Mario Pino
Hard Spun

David Flores
Liquidity

Stewart Elliott
Teuflesberg

Javier Castellano
Bwana Bull

Cornelio Velasquez
Nobiz Like Shobiz

Ramon Dominquez
Sam P.

Edgar Prado
Scat Daddy

Mike Smith
Tiago

John Velazquez
Circular Quay

Kent Desormeaux
Stormello

Garrett Gomez
Any Given Saturday

Rafael Bejarano
Dominican

Corey Nakatani
Great Hunter

46

If there is a moment on Kentucky Derby Day that is guaranteed to create a lump in the throat, generate a tear in the corner of the eye, or make the heart pound, it is this one. The riders are up, resplendent in their respective stable colors, and most in the throng of spectators under the venerable Twin Spires add their voices to the familiar chorus.

"Weep no more, my lady. Oh weep no more today!
We will sing one song for the old Kentucky home,
For the old Kentucky home far away."

race
the

Street Sense (second from left in blue and yellow silks) breaks alertly from post 7 and is close to the leaders in the opening strides of Derby 133, but would soon trail all but one of his rivals by the time the field completed its first run down the long Churchill Downs homestretch.

It takes roughly two minutes and a couple of seconds, give or take a second or two, for a top quality 3-year-old Thoroughbred to find his or her way past as many as 19 rivals to win the Kentucky Derby. But inside those roughly 120 seconds are several moments that possess potential for high drama – and few are more critical than the start of the great race.

start

While the starting gate is as familiar a racing fixture as the finish line to most racing fans, those mechanical devices did not come into use in American racing until 1930. Before the introduction of the gate, horses lined up for the start – as pictured here in the 1918 Kentucky Derby won by Exterminator – and left at the signal of the crack of the starter's whip. If a start was deemed less than perfect, the horses would be called back for another try.

It can be argued many renewals of the Kentucky Derby have been won or lost in the opening strides of its daunting mile and a quarter. Possible pitfalls that could end, or at least seriously damage, the hopes of contenders in the opening yards of the great race include such mishaps as a slow or awkward start, a collision with a rival that failed to maintain a straight path out of the gate, or a quicker than planned break that makes a contender part of a contested duel for the early lead.

There would be no new tales of nightmare starts in the 2007 Kentucky Derby to add to that particular volume of Derby lore. The start of the race would provide no significant excuse for any of the horses that would fall short in their bid to win the 133rd "Run for the Roses."

first pass

Although the maximum field of 20 horses entered the starting gate for the 2007 Kentucky Derby, the start of the race was as flawless as any could hope when the doors flew open at 6:16 p.m. (EDT). Hard Spun and jockey Mario Pino, an accomplished Maryland-based jockey riding in his first Derby at the age of 45, had turned in a sizzling workout early in Derby Week and were expected to grab the early advantage – and did.

Pushed early by fellow speedsters Stormello, Cowtown Cat and Teuflesberg, Hard Spun would hold a narrow lead as the field made its first pass by the stands. James Tafel's homebred Street Sense, a narrow favorite at odds of $4.90-to-1, dropped back after breaking from post seven and was guided to the inside for a rail-hugging journey by jockey Calvin Borel. Curlin, the second choice of the fans at $5-to-1, had been close to the front in earlier races but did not break sharply. Forced to steady slightly in traffic under jockey Robby Albarado during the first eighth of a mile, the muscular chestnut trailed a dozen horses as the Kentucky Derby 133 field navigated its run to the first turn.

A jockey's judgement during the initial run down Churchill Downs' famed homestretch can be a critical component of their mount's performance in the Derby. It is a balancing act, both literally and figuratively, required of every jockey to make the correct split-second decisions during the race that can affect its outcome.

Here jockey Mario Pino, a picture of focused concentration aboard Hard Spun led the charge to get clear running over his pursuing rivals and establish a narrow advantage on that initial run down the stretch in the veteran rider's first bid for racing's most coveted prize.

Eventual runner-up Hard Spun led the field of 20 horses around the first turn in Kentucky Derby 133, while speedy rivals Stormello and Teuflesberg were forced to lose ground and run wide. Eventual winner Street Sense is on the rail (upper right) and trails all in the field but Imawildandcrazyguy.

first turn

The first, or Clubhouse, turn has been the scene of considerable Derby drama through the years. Horses no longer face the prospect of dangerously close contact with spectators, as was the case in the 1931 Derby won by Greentree Stable's Twenty Grand (above). Infield spectators could literally reach out and touch the 12-horse field as they rushed past.

The most famous victim of first turn pitfalls was Native Dancer, racing's first star of the television age and a heavy favorite for the 1953 Derby. After being "roughed" on that first turn he would be flying at the finish, only to fall a head short of catching the winner, Dark Star. That Derby was the only loss suffered by Native Dancer in 22 career races.

This unusual view of the Kentucky Derby 133 field as it entered the first turn offers a perspective similar to that of jockey Calvin Borel and Street Sense, far left, as they lagged far behind in the early going. Displaying his ground-saving tactical trademark, Borel eased Street Sense to the rail where the jockey would patiently wait until making his winning move.

After navigating the potential mayhem on the first turn, the run down the roughly one-quarter mile back-stretch straightaway could be the only part of the Kentucky Derby's mile and a quarter that would even remotely be considered as an opportunity of a "breather." And that is only the case if your horse was not among those vying for the lead, or had been forced to deviate from a normal running style by the dynamics of the only 20-horse field he or she would ever face.

Hard Spun, running fast, but comfortably under Pino, started to edge clear – first a length, then two – from his closest competitors. Street Sense and Borel continued to trail all but one horse but were saving precious ground while skimming the rail.

"He'll do anything for you," Borel said later of Street Sense. "He'll put you in a spot where you want to be at any time and then relax."

By the end of the backstretch run, Borel had let Street Sense out a notch. He was unimpeded on the rail and quickly advancing through the field. Horse and rider were a half-mile from racing's most hallowed ground: the Kentucky Derby winner's circle on the first Saturday in May.

The pacesetting Hard Spun begins to expand his advantage with about five furlongs to run as he leads his rivals down the backstretch against the backdrop of the famed Twin Spires of Churchill Downs.

back stretch

"He'll put you in a spot where you want to be at any time and then relax."

— Calvin Borel

As the field made its way past the cheering crowd along the backstretch, it sped beneath a banner that heralded the introduction of TwinSpires.com. Launched just before the 2007 Derby under the leadership of new Churchill Downs CEO Bob Evans, TwinSpires.com is an

advance deposit wagering service that enabled fans to watch and wager on the Derby, Churchill Downs races, and racing from other popular tracks. This innovative blend of technology and tradition reflected another step in the corporate growth of Churchill Downs and its premier event.

As the Derby field navigated the far turn, left, Borel continued to encounter clear sailing along the rail and began to pull within striking distance with three furlongs remaining. He had yet to ask Street Sense for his greatest trait. Horsemen call it "turn of foot." In basketball, it would be an explosive first step that leaves a defender seemingly nailed to the floor. In racing, it's instant acceleration – an incredible weapon in an unwieldy field of 20 horses where openings can materialize – then vanish – in an instant. With Hard Spun in his cross-hairs, below, Calvin Borel and Street Sense took aim on the lead. The veteran jockey, who had never finished higher than eighth in four previous Derby rides was about to smell the roses.

far turn

stretch

When the field in any Kentucky Derby turns for home, they are confronted by 1,234 $^1/_2$ feet of real estate – the distance between the quarter pole at the top of the home stretch and the finish line that lay beneath the shadow of the century-old Twin Spires.

That stretch of track, dubbed "Heart-break Lane," has seen countless dreams soar before crashing in the final yards of the most demanding test of a young horse's career. These Thoroughbreds, with rare exceptions, have never run farther than 1 $^1/_8$ miles in their previous starts – an eighth of a mile shorter than the Derby distance. And never have they faced the deafening roar from nearly 160,000 screaming fans – a cacophony that comes crashing down on the field from both the stands and the infield when they straighten away for the run to the wire.

After surging past the pacesetting Hard Spun, Street Sense opened a clear lead in the homestretch of Kentucky Derby 133. He then returned to his comfort zone along the rail as only a few hundred yards remained of the Derby's demanding mile and a quarter distance.

Street Sense and Calvin Borel were rolling after a journey so devoid of traffic problems that they needed to leave their inside path only once during the entire running of the race.

"I stayed on the fence to about the quarter pole and I went around one horse after that," recalled Borel. "After that, you know, it was just a matter of how far he went, because I knew when I asked him, he'd go."

Would he ever. Street Sense collared Hard Spun with just over an eighth of a mile remaining in the Derby and quickly drew clear. Borel pivoted slightly in the saddle during that final furlong and looked back over his right shoulder in search of a late

threat. Then, and only then, did the 40-year-old Louisiana native allow himself to acknowledge a notion that had been nearly unthinkable.

"I looked under my arm and saw I was two or three lengths in front and there was no way he (Hard Spun) was going to beat me, and I knew then," said Borel.

A sequence of photographic images, left, captures Kentucky Derby winner Street Sense as he draws away through the stretch and strides toward the finish line of Derby 133. Jockey Calvin Borel keeps the 3-year-old focused on his task as the colt flashes past the infield tote board in the final yards of Churchill Downs' long homestretch. Below, Borel urges Street Sense near the finish and the colt, his ears pinned back in a show of determination and focus, responds with his best in the 133rd "Run for the Roses."

Through most of his quarter-century in the saddle, Borel had looked on the Derby as racing's ultimate dream, but it took Street Sense to make it a dream come true. He saved every inch of ground for nearly a mile, and responded with his typically explosive acceleration when his rider asked for his best. The colt would hit the finish line 2 ¹/₄-lengths in front of Hard Spun in a Kentucky Derby that had essentially boiled down to a two-horse affair. The winning time was 2:02.17.

The previously unbeaten but inexperienced Curlin, who was making only his fourth career start

Photojournalists from wire services and publications from around the globe focused their lenses from assigned spots along the rail in an effort to capture a perfect image of the Kentucky Derby's signature moment as the victorious Street Sense flashed past the Twin Spires. Within minutes the first winner's photograph was distributed via Associated Press outlets, and Street Sense was on his way to new status as a household name in American sport.

after a belated racing debut in February, overcame early

trouble and gained a career's worth of racing experience

as he rallied to finish third, 5 ³/₄-lengths behind the

runner-up. Imawildandcrazyguy, the only horse that

trailed Street Sense through most of the race, rallied

in the stretch to end up in fourth.

Calvin Borel's victory aboard Street Sense forever placed him in the company of riding legends like Isaac Murphy, Bill Shoemaker, Eddie Arcaro, Jimmy Winkfield and Earl Sande, and confirmed his mount as the successor to the beloved but star-crossed 2006 Derby winner Barbaro on a roster of Derby heroes that include Secretariat, Citation, War Admiral, and Affirmed.

"It's the greatest moment of your life to win the Kentucky Derby."

— Calvin Borel

When Calvin Borel crossed the finish line well in front of 19 beaten rivals, the third largest crowd to witness a Kentucky Derby keenly zeroed in on the jockey as he stood high in the irons and repeatedly jabbed his right fist into the air in a display of pure exhilaration and emotion. This spontaneous and joyous celebration of his career-defining moment turned him into an instant highlight on ESPN's SportsCenter and made the quiet Cajun a national sports star.

Borel had come about as far as one could travel from the day he had first climbed into a saddle as an eight-year-old at a Louisiana bush track, and now joined the elite ranks of American riding talent – he had won the Kentucky Derby, the biggest race of them all.

In the moments after Street Sense won the Kentucky Derby, during that slow and deliberate gallop that would end in the winner's circle with a blanket of roses being placed over his withers, it became clear that the result of the race and the celebration it inspired were far from typical.

As emotionally overwhelming as a Kentucky Derby victory must be, few jockeys in its previous 133 runnings of the Derby were as ebullient during the jog back to the winner's circle as Borel. And the reaction of the crowd to Borel's outpouring of pure and unfiltered bliss could well have been unprecedented. "It's the greatest moment of your life to win the Kentucky Derby," Borel said. "It's the greatest thing in the world to me.

As Borel made his way to the winner's circle aboard Street Sense, he let his tears flow freely as he bathed in what could well be an unprecedented show of affection from the massive crowd gathered under the Twin Spires.

A victory in the Kentucky Derby is a dream sought and shared by owners, trainers and jockeys from all parts of the globe. Contenders in recent Derby renewals of the great race have hailed from all sections of the United States, as well as Canada, Ireland, England, Dubai and Japan. But if one wanted to find the winner of the 2007 "Run for the Roses," all that was needed was a stroll to Barn 26 on the Churchill Downs backside.

Jockey Calvin Borel rewards an appreciative Street Sense with a splash of cool water, above, as the bay colt was surrounded by an admiring mix of media and fans, left, moments before entering the Kentucky Derby winner's circle at Churchill Downs. Congratulating the victorious jockey Calvin Borel was fellow rider Javier Castellano, lower right corner, who finished 15th aboard Bwana Bull.

The 2007 Kentucky Derby, won by James Tafel's Street Sense, was witnessed by a gathering of 156,635. Along with the audience that gathers at Churchill Downs each year for America's oldest continuously held sports event, millions more watch the television broadcast of the race on NBC Sports. Its grand legacy is celebrated throughout the world on the first Saturday in May, the traditional day of the great race.

On the tradition-soaked grounds of the Louisville track, Nafzger had sculpted a Kentucky Derby champion in Street Sense. Not since W.C. Partee's Lil E. Tee won the race in 1992 for Churchill-based trainer Lynn Whiting and

local riding king Pat Day had there been such reason for local fans to cheer when their track was at the center of the racing world's brightest stage. James Tafel's Street Sense, Carl Nafzger and Calvin Borel won the 133rd Kentucky Derby for the home team, and on this Derby Day, it seemed that all in the crowd, and even the Queen of England, cheered for their heroes like lifelong Louisvillians.

ENDING THE JINX

The Kentucky Derby victory by Street Sense ended a run of bad luck – some would call it a "jinx" – in Americas greatest race by horses that had earned championship honors at the age of two and won the Breeders' Cup Juvenile six months prior to Derby Day.

The last juvenile champion to return to win the Kentucky Derby the following spring was the great Spectacular Bid, a member of racing's Hall of Fame who was the champion 2-year-old in 1978 and won the Derby's roses in '79.

But until this year's victory by Street Sense, no horse that had won the Breeders' Cup Juvenile had ever tasted success in the Derby. Chief's Crown had won the first running of the Juvenile in 1984, but finished third to Spend A Buck – only to reverse the order of finish in the Derby with Spend A Buck winning and Chief's Crown taking the show spot.

As Spend A Buck had emphatically proven, participation in the Breeders' Cup Juvenile was no impediment to success on Derby Day. Two other Juvenile also-rans – Alysheba and Sea Hero – failed to win the Juvenile, but bounced back to earn the roses on Derby Day the following spring.

When the two-year-old Street Sense romped to a 10-length victory in the Breeders' Cup Juvenile at Churchill Downs, he clinched championship honors in his age group. When he won the Derby six months later, he dispatched both alleged jinxes in one fell swoop.

The victory by Street Sense in the Kentucky Derby defied recent history and what had been conventional wisdom on how to best prepare a 3-year-old Thoroughbred to win America's greatest race.

Street Sense also ignored conventional wisdom as he won the demanding 1 1/4-mile test at Churchill Downs on the first Saturday in May off of only two prep races. The last horse to win the Derby off such a limited schedule was the David Cross-trained Sunny's Halo in 1983. Before that the feat had been accomplished by Jet Pilot, who won the 1947 Derby for trainer Tom Smith of Seabiscuit fame.

Street Sense had taken a bit longer than Nafzger had expected to return from a brief winter break, a delay that prompted his trainer to rethink the champion's road to the Derby. The plan devised by Nafzger would take Street Sense first to Florida's Tampa Bay Downs, where he would narrowly win the Tampa Bay Derby in mid-March, with a final prep race over Keeneland's synthetic Polytrack surface in April's Toyota Blue Grass Stakes, where he would finish a close second to Dominican.

"There were two races because the horse already had five," said Nafzger in explaining the schedule. "He had already learned his lessons. It was a matter of getting fit and getting his timing. If two's not enough to win it, three won't win it either."

Besides Street Sense, the roster of other 3-year-olds with pre-Derby schedules that consisted of just two preps is an impressive group that includes 1937 Derby winner War Admiral, pictured below, Shut Out (1942), Count Fleet (1943) and Hoop Jr. (1945). War Admiral and Count Fleet went on to sweep the Triple Crown and are enshrined in the National Museum of Racing and Hall of Fame in Saratoga Springs, NY.

For jockey Calvin Borel and owner James Tafel, this Derby would provide their first opportunity to relish the scent of the Derby's fabled roses. For trainer Carl Nafzger, Street Sense provided a second opportunity to live racing's most cherished dream. His 1990 victory with Unbridled for owner Frances Genter had instantly made the veteran trainer a part of Derby lore. Nafzger's second Derby victory put him in elite company, as he joined the small club of two-time winners that includes Nick Zito, Lucien Laurin, Laz Barrera, Woody Stephens, Charlie Whittingham, H.A. "Jimmy" Jones, Horatio Luro, LeRoy Jolley, Henry Forrest, James Rowe, Sr., and John McGinty.

Although 17 years separated Nafzger's two Kentucky Derby triumphs, he said on the morning after the victory by Street Sense that the emotions generated by the victory in 2007 were identical to those he experienced when Unbridled gave him that first scent of roses.

"It's the same – you never get tired of winning the Kentucky Derby," he said. "You never get tired of reaching the pinnacle. And that's what it is when you're in the Derby. You've reached the higher pinnacle. Not you, but in history, and life, and accomplishments – you've done something. It's hard to do."

Nafzger, who in 2006 had cut back his daily training activity but stopped just short of retirement, displayed a maestro's touch in preparing Street Sense to win the Derby off just a pair of prep races. But Nafzger was not about to believe that his training regimen had won the roses. The credit, he said, belonged to Street Sense, as the horse carried him – along with Tafel, Borel and everyone else – into the Derby winner's circle.

"You've reached the higher pinnacle."

— Carl Nafzger

The official gathering of the Street Sense team in that hallowed ground at Churchill Downs included Nafzger's wife Wanda, his constant companion, assistant Ian Wilkes and wife Tracey, and all the members of the extended family that calls the Nafzger barn "home" each day.

But reveling most in the moment was Jim Tafel, a longtime client and friend who had built a successful racing and breeding operation with the winning trainer. He and his wife Gus, their family and friends, all stood in that rarified air surrounding their rose-draped champion. There, in the glow of a warm Kentucky sun, they would come to the gratifying realization that out of an American foal crop totaling more than 37,000, Street Sense stood alone as the winner of the 2007 Kentucky Derby.

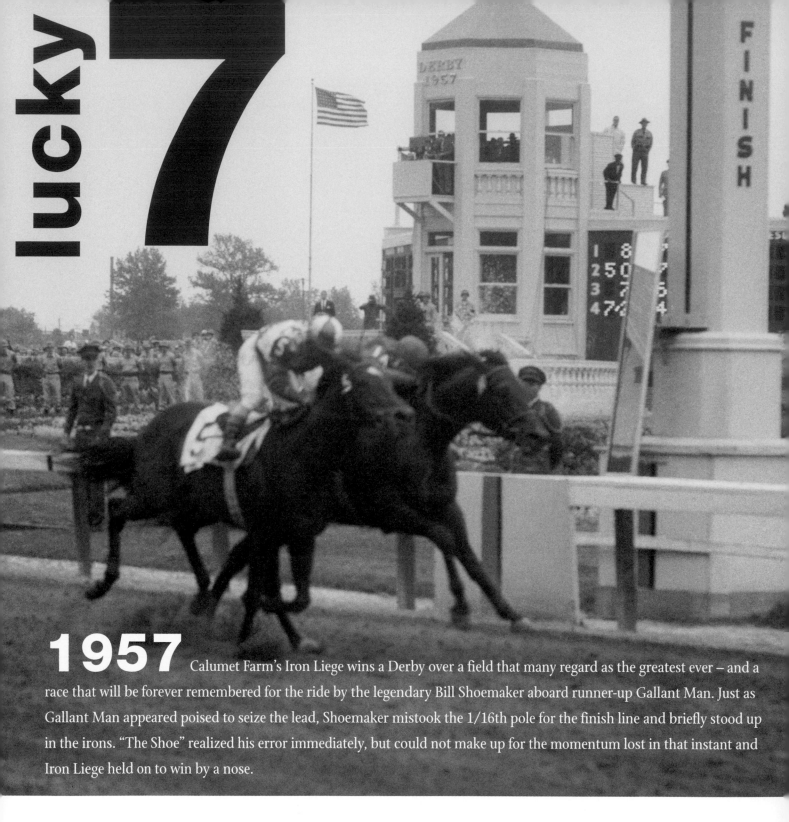

lucky 7

1957 Calumet Farm's Iron Liege wins a Derby over a field that many regard as the greatest ever – and a race that will be forever remembered for the ride by the legendary Bill Shoemaker aboard runner-up Gallant Man. Just as Gallant Man appeared poised to seize the lead, Shoemaker mistook the 1/16th pole for the finish line and briefly stood up in the irons. "The Shoe" realized his error immediately, but could not make up for the momentum lost in that instant and Iron Liege held on to win by a nose.

History will ultimately decide if Street Sense is indeed a very special Thoroughbred. His striking come-from-behind victory under jockey Calvin Borel was one of the most memorable rallies in Derby history, and it continued a run of remarkable Derbys in years that end with the numeral seven. Call them "The Lucky 7's," if you will - lucky for the racing fans who witnessed this run of magnificent performances over the last fifty years that are now a part of Derby lore.

1967

Longshot Proud Clarion won the race under jockey Bobby Ussery, but this Derby may be best remembered as the one that the Hall of Famer Damascus lost. Damascus finished a poor third in that Derby, but would win the Preakness and Belmont Stakes to cap a "Horse of the Year" campaign. The loss by Damascus is a reminder that being the best horse does not guarantee success on Kentucky Derby Day.

1977

Unbeaten Seattle Slew overcame a poor start to score a dominating victory in the Derby for jockey Jean Cruguet and trainer Billy Turner. The dark bay colt would go on to sweep the Preakness and Belmont Stakes for owners Mickey and Karen Taylor to become the first and only Triple Crown winner with a perfect record. Seattle Slew would later sire a Kentucky Derby winner in Swale (1984).

1987

Alysheba and jockey Chris McCarron turned in one of the most remarkable athletic feats in Kentucky Derby history when he clipped heels with front-running Bet Twice in deep stretch and nearly fell – but somehow regained his balance and stride and went on to win the roses. The son of 1978 Derby runner-up Alydar would end his career as racing's all-time earnings leader.

1997

Silver Charm under jockey Gary Stevens gives three-time Derby winning trainer Bob Baffert his first Derby victory. The gray colt owned by Bob and Beverly Lewis was one of the most popular Derby winners of recent years. With his narrow victory in the $5 million Dubai Gold Cup Silver Charm become the first Derby winner to win outside of the U.S. since 1973 Derby champion Secretariat.

1962 DECIDEDLY 1963 CHATEAUGAY 1964 NORTHERN DANCER 1965 LUCKY DEBONAIR 1966 KAUAI KING 1967 PROUD CLARION 1968 FORWARD PASS 1969 MAJESTIC PRINCE 1970 DUST COMMANDER 1971 CANONERO II 1972 RIVA RIDGE 1973 SECRETARIAT 1974 CANNONADE 1975 FOOLISH PLEASURE 1976 BOLD FORBES 1977 SEATTLE SLEW 1978 AFFIRMED 1979 SPECTACULAR BID 1980 GENUINE RISK 1981 PLEASANT COLONY 1982 GATO DEL SOL 1983 SUNNY'S HALO 1984 SWALE 1985 SPEND A BUCK 1986 FERDINAND 1987 ALYSHEBA 1988 WINNING COLORS 1989 SUNDAY SILENCE 1990 UNBRIDLED 1991 STRIKE THE GOLD 1992 LIL E. TEE 1993 SEA HERO 1994 GO FOR GIN 1995 THUNDER GULCH 1996 GRINDSTONE 1997 SILVER CHARM 1998 REAL QUIET 1999 CHARISMATIC 2000 FUSAICHI PEGASUS 2001 MONARCHOS 2002 WAR EMBLEM 2003 FUNNY CIDE 2004 SMARTY JONES 2005 GIACOMO 2006 BARBARO 2007 STREET SENSE

official

jockey

Calvin Borel

The segment of the American public that rarely follows Thoroughbred racing beyond the Kentucky Derby, the Triple Crown and the Breeders' Cup World Championships had little reason to know Calvin Borel. But all that changed on the first Saturday in May in 2007.

The native of St. Martinville, La. had started his career, like so many riding stars from his home, by riding in races at unsanctioned "bush tracks" at the age of eight. As a professional, he had toiled mostly at tracks in Louisiana, Arkansas and Kentucky before, as Borel's agent Jerry Hissam put it, he "became an overnight sensation after 25 years" when he won the Kentucky Derby aboard Street Sense.

The previous 12 months under Churchill Downs' famed Twin Spires had been extraordinary for Borel. He had scored a breakthrough victory aboard Street Sense in the $2 million Bessemer Trust Breeders' Cup Juvenile at Churchill Downs. That win clinched an Eclipse Award for Street Sense as 2-year-old champion and provided Borel his first triumph in the Breeders' Cup World Championships. To that point it was the greatest victory of his career.

Known for his remarkable energy and work ethic, fellow jockeys and trainers had long loved to tell stories about Borel and how, on mornings after a big victories, he could be found back in the saddle before dawn when the track opened for training. He had worked closely throughout his career with his brother, trainer Cecil Borel, and it was never a surprise to walk past the Borel barn at 5 a.m. and see Calvin, pitchfork in hand, mucking stalls for his brother before climbing aboard several horses for workouts and gallops during training hours. It's a work ethic he carries with him to this day. Borel's relentless drive was reflected in his extraordinary penchant for ground-saving, and sometimes daring, rides that earned the 40-year-old veteran jockey the sobriquet "Calvin Bo-Rail."

At a Kentucky Derby notable for the presence of the Queen of England in her first visit to historic Churchill Downs, the most memorable character on this memorable Derby stage was clearly Borel.

Borel, with fiancée Lisa Funk at this side, wept as he stood on the victory stand. After the race, he paid tribute to his brother, who had pushed him throughout his career, and their father, who had died three years earlier.

"I always dreamed about winning this race," said Borel. "It's the greatest moment in your life to win the Kentucky Derby."

As amazing as the realization of his Derby dream had been, nothing could have prepared him for the telephone call he received the next day from the White House. Borel and his fiancée were invited to Washington, D.C. for a white-tie state dinner held by President George W. Bush and First Lady Laura Bush in honor of Queen Elizabeth II.

Borel surely might have dreamed of winning the Derby, but he could never have imagined that his victory would lead to being greeted at the White House by two of the world's most important and visible leaders. But the Kentucky Derby has always possessed a special romance that seemed to bestow Derby glory on those who deserve it most. From the smiles on the faces of the grooms, the legion in the infield, the nattily attired residents on Millionaires Row, to Her Majesty the Queen, it was clear that the Derby had bestowed its magic on a most deserving recipient in Calvin Borel.

Carl Nafzger

Trainer Carl Nafzger has always done things his own way – which befits a native Texan-turned-Kentuckian who was once ranked as the third-best rodeo bull rider in the world before he decided to give up bovine pursuits for a life in the equine world.

Nafzger's distinctive style earned him a second victory in the Kentucky Derby when Street Sense won the roses in 2007 for old friend and client James Tafel. His previous success on Derby Day had come with Unbridled in 1990 – a moment that gave the trainer a special spot in Derby history as ABC Sports cameras caught him giving 92-year-old owner Mrs. Frances Genter a vivid and joyous personal call of the race as her only Derby starter in more than 60 years in racing took the coveted roses.

Nafzger's stubborn embrace of the methods he had developed over the years kept jockey Calvin Borel in the saddle aboard his star on the road to the Derby. His loyalty to the journeyman rider dissuaded agents of higher profile jockeys from seeking the mount on Street Sense. Those agents knew better – Borel was Nafzger's man and he would stick with him.

Nafzger's instincts also convinced him to bring Street Sense into the Derby off of an unorthodox schedule that included just two prep races as a 3-year-old. But he believed in his methods, his rider and – most of all – his horse.

"This horse took us here," said Nafzger. "I've got all the faith in the world in this horse and I can't say enough about him."

Nafzger's Kentucky Derby victory with Street Sense came in the twilight of a distinguished training career. He had edged toward retirement when he handed the training of most of his horses over to longtime assistant Ian Wilkes in early 2006, but Nafzger had continued to condition horses owned by Tafel and Bentley Smith, Genter's son-in-law. Those few remaining horses included a promising young colt named Street Sense.

On the morning after Street Sense won the Kentucky Derby, the iconoclastic Nafzger continued to march to his distinctive rhythm. While nearly every other Derby winner in memory received a few days away from the track after winning the biggest race of their lives, Street Sense was out of the barn and on the track for a one mile jog just hours after the Derby Day crowd had bathed him in applause.

And who, you might ask, was the last Derby winner to take that victory lap on the morning after the race? It was Unbridled who adhered to that routine, with Nafzger looking on, exactly 17 years earlier.

THE FAMILY WILKES

The Street Sense team could more accurately be described as a family. This applies specifically to the husband and wife team of Ian and Tracey Wilkes – key members of the Nafzger barn.

Aside from an early three-year return to their native Australia, Ian and Tracey have been with the Nafzger team since 1989. Ian was the exercise rider for 1990 Derby winner Unbridled, and the onetime student now trains horses for most of the clients once served by his mentor.

Tracey's contributions come in the saddle during training hours, and she frequently galloped and worked Street Sense. Her only lament was that the Derby winner seemed a bit too enthusiastic about lessons learned from jockey Calvin Borel. "Calvin's got him trained," said Tracey (holding roses below). "He gets a little too close to the rail for my taste."

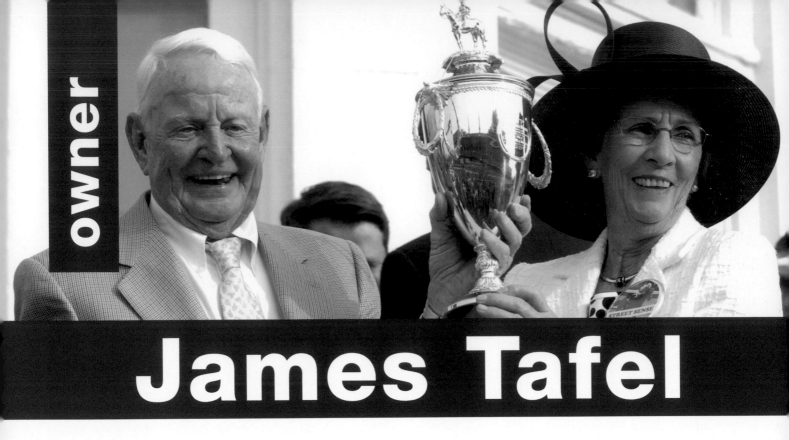

James Tafel

After James Tafel retired in 1983 from a successful business career as board chairman and chief executive officer of Dun & Bradstreet Technical Publishing, Co., he began to dabble in horse ownership as a member of partnerships. From that seed grew a racing and breeding venture that brought the 83-year-old Tafel to the hallowed ground of the Kentucky Derby winner's circle on May 5, 2007 as the owner and breeder of Street Sense, winner of the 133rd Kentucky Derby.

Through many of those years, Tafel – who was born in Pittsburgh but now lives in Chicago with wife Gus – has employed Carl Nafzger as his primary trainer. Their partnership had enjoyed success with the champion filly Banshee Breeze on its list of stakes winners. Bedazzle was not the most notable of the horses bred and raced by Tafel and trained by Nafzger – she won four of 22 races and just under $200,000 in her career. But when she launched her first season of a new career in the breeding shed, Tafel wanted to send her to a first-year stallion named Street Cry, a winner of the Dubai World Cup who had impressed Tafel with a victory in the Stephen Foster Handicap at Churchill Downs. But he encountered some resistance in that plan from Nafzger and other advisers.

"Some of my friends weren't too enthusiastic about the breeding, because it was using an unproven stallion with an unproven broodmare," said Tafel. "So I guess that's a bunch of nonsense that produced Street Sense."

"When we got down to Bedazzle, he showed his veto power right quick," Nafzger recalled. "He said, 'Guys, think what you want to and do what you want to, but I've got the most votes, and we're going to Street Cry.' So that was the vote right there."

The product of Tafel's inspiration was Street Sense, who would earn an Eclipse Award as the champion 2-year-old of 2006 when he scored a record 10-length victory in the Breeders' Cup Juvenile over his home track at Churchill Downs. He then became the first horse in history to sweep the Breeders' Cup race and the Kentucky Derby with his come-from-behind triumph under jockey Calvin Borel on the first Saturday in May.

"The epitome for anybody in the horse business or in a racing career is to have a horse that's won the Kentucky Derby," said Tafel. "You've got 20 horses in there and a lot of things can happen. Bad things can happen to good horses. Fortunately, Calvin kept us out of trouble and got us across that finish line first. So it's a real thrill."

Kentucky Derby Presented by Yum! Brands– Grade 1
Purse: $ 2,000,000 Guaranteed

10th Race Churchill Downs – May 5, 2007

Stakes. Purse $ 2,000,000. 3 yo. 1 1/4 Miles Dirt Track: Fast

P#	Horse (Purse Earned)	Sex/Age	Wgt	Med	Eqp	Odds	PP	1/4	1/2	3/4	1m	Str	Fin	Jockey
7	Street Sense ($1,450,000)	c3	126	L	f	4.90	7	$18^{1/2}$	19^5	17^{hd}	3^{hd}	1^1	$1^{2\,1/4}$	C H Borel
8	Hard Spun ($400,000)	c3	126	L		10.00	8	1^{hd}	1^1	1^2	1^3	2^4	$2^{5\,3/4}$	M G Pino
2	Curlin ($200,000)	c3	126	L		5.00	2	$13^{1/2}$	$13^{2\,1/2}$	$14^{1\,1/2}$	8^{hd}	6^1	$3^{1/2}$	R Albarado
5	Imawildandcrazyguy ($100,000)	g3	126	L	b	28.90	5	20	20	20	$16^{1/2}$	$11^{1\,1/2}$	$4^{1/2}$	M Guidry
1	Sedgefield ($60,000)	c3	126	L	b	58.60	1	$5^{1/2}$	$5^{1\,1/2}$	3^{hd}	$2^{1/2}$	3^{hd}	5^{nk}	J R Leparoux
16	Circular Quay	c3	126	L		11.40	16	19^3	18^1	16^{hd}	$13^{1/2}$	$8^{1/2}$	$6^{3/4}$	J R Velazquez
15	Tiago	c3	126	L		14.80	15	17^{hd}	$17^{1/2}$	18^4	15^1	12^{hd}	$7^{1/2}$	M E Smith
18	Any Given Saturday	c3	126	L		13.60	18	$8^{1/2}$	$9^{1\,1/2}$	9^1	4^{hd}	$4^{2\,1/2}$	$8^{2\,1/2}$	G K Gomez
13	Sam P.	c3	126	L		43.70	13	$12^{2\,1/2}$	12^1	12^1	7^{hd}	$7^{1\,1/2}$	$9^{1\,1/2}$	R A Dominguez
12	Nobiz Like Shobiz	c3	126	L	b	10.40	12	6^{hd}	$6^{1\,1/2}$	6^1	5^{hd}	5^{hd}	10^3	C H Velasquez
19	Dominican	g3	126	L		24.90	19	$11^{1\,1/2}$	10^{hd}	10^{hd}	$10^{1/2}$	$14^{2\,1/2}$	11^{nk}	R Bejarano
3	Zanjero	c3	126	L		36.00	3	16^2	15^3	13^{hd}	$11^{1/2}$	$10^{1/2}$	$12^{2\,3/4}$	S Bridgmohan
20	Great Hunter	c3	126	L	b	25.30	20	$9^{1/2}$	$11^{2\,1/2}$	$11^{1/2}$	$6^{1/2}$	9^{hd}	$13^{1\,3/4}$	C S Nakatani
9	Liquidity	c3	126	L		40.00	9	$10^{1/2}$	$8^{1/2}$	$7^{1/2}$	9^{hd}	13^1	$14^{3/4}$	D R Flores
11	Bwana Bull	c3	126	L	b	50.50	11	14^2	14^{hd}	15^1	$19^{1/2}$	16^2	15^1	J Castellano
4	Storm in May	c3	126	L		27.20	4	$15^{1\,1/2}$	16^{hd}	$19^{2\,1/2}$	18^2	$15^{1/2}$	$16^{11\,1/2}$	J C Leyva
10	Teuflesberg	c3	126	L		51.90	10	4^1	$3^{1/2}$	$2^{1/2}$	12^{hd}	$17^{1/2}$	$17^{2\,3/4}$	S Elliott
14	Scat Daddy	c3	126	L		7.20	14	7^1	7^{hd}	8^{hd}	20	20	$18^{6\,1/4}$	E S Prado
17	Stormello	c3	126	L	b	44.80	17	2^{hd}	4^1	5^{hd}	$14^{1\,1/2}$	$18^{1\,1/2}$	$19^{7\,1/4}$	K J Desormeaux
6	Cowtown Cat	c3	126	L		19.80	6	$3^{1/2}$	$2^{1/2}$	4^1	$17^{1\,1/2}$	$19^{1/2}$	20	F Jara

Off Time: 6:16		**Time Of Race:** 22.96 46.26 1:11.13 1:37.04 2:02.17			
Start: Good For All	**WON:** Driving	**Temp:** 68°	**Weather:** Cloudy		

Total W/P/S Pool: $49,564,991

Mutuel Payoffs

7 Street Sense	11.80 6.40 4.60	
8 Hard Spun	9.80 7.00	
2 Curlin	5.60	

$2.00	Exacta (7–8)	$101.80	Total Pool: $22,764,587
$2.00	Trifecta (7–8–2)	$440.00	Total Pool: $27,601,096
$2.00	Superfecta (7–8–2–5)	$29,046.40	Total Pool: $8,979,962
$2.00	Daily Double (7–7)	$87.00	Total Pool: $768,866
$2.00	Daily Double (OAKS/DERBY 11–7)	$23.80	Total Pool: $2,309,972
$2.00	Pick 3 (7–7–7)	$927.60	Total Pool: $1,275,236
$2.00	Pick 4 (3–7–7–7)	$4,783.40	Total Pool: $2,174,027
$2.00	Pick 6 (7–7–3–7–7–7)	$1,263.00	Total Pool: $0
$2.00	Pick 6 (7–7–3–7–7–7)	$231,225.40	Total Pool: $1,429,995
$2.00	Future Wager (POOL 1 – 22)	$22.80	Total Pool: $520,688
$2.00	Future Wager (POOL 2 – 20)	$18.20	Total Pool: $379,613
$2.00	Future Wager (POOL 3 – 20)	$15.40	Total Pool: $465,123

Winner: Street Sense, dk b/ c 3 , by Street Cry (IRE)–Bedazzle, by Dixieland Band
Bred in Kentucky by James Tafel

STREET SENSE, reserved immediately after the start as the field came away in good order, relaxed nicely, reached the rail before going a furlong and settled well off the pace, began picking up horses approaching the far turn, got through cleanly inside, split foes two or three wide at the quarter–mile ground, moved three wide to go after pace–setting HARD SPUN, took over, opened a clear advantage at the furlong grounds when roused sharply left–handed, then, with the rider glancing back and changing hands with the stick, continued resolutely. HARD SPUN worked his way in two wide to vie for the lead early, gained the lead soon after going a quarter while racing in hand, edged clear entering the backstretch while carefully handled, increased his advantage to be well clear into the upper stretch, bobbled leaving the eighth pole, angled outside of STREET SENSE in the late going and wasn't a match for that one as second best. CURLIN, steadied lightly during the opening eighth while between rivals near the inside, was unhurried to the end of the backstretch between horses, continued between rivals when advancing into the stretch, made a bold run five wide approaching the final furlong but couldn't threaten the top two. IMAWILDANDCRAZYGUY, outrun four wide for seven furlongs, moved between rivals approaching the final quarter, swung out ten wide entering the stretch and made up some ground. SEDGEFIELD, forwardly placed near the inside from the outset, raced within easy striking distance into the upper stretch and came up empty. CIRCULAR QUAY raced far back five or six wide from early on, bumped for a stride with STORMELLO leaving the five–sixteenths pole, then improved position slightly while not a threat. TIAGO, outrun early, angled to the inside on the far turn, rallied along the rail approaching the stretch, continued three abreast when straightened for the drive and passed tired rivals. ANY GIVEN SATURDAY, never far back and between foes four wide, launched a bid midway down the backstretch, came out causing crowding while bumping with SCAT DADDY nearing the far turn, made an earnest run five wide between horses approaching the final quarter but flattened out when straightened for the drive. SAM P., unhurried for a half, made mild move six wide approaching the stretch but failed to continue. NOBIZ LIKE SHOBIZ, well placed while tracking the leaders from between horses, moved menacingly approaching the final quarter but faltered. DOMINICAN, in contention while between horses, was shuffled back in tight while bumping with GREAT HUNTER nearing the far turn and was finished nearing the stretch. ZANJERO settled near the inside, advanced steadily between calls on the far turn, had to steady when lacking room, was with the winner while outside that one, steadied again before the quarter–pole and had no further response. GREAT HUNTER, bumped with DOMINICAN in the early going, raced six or seven wide along the backstretch, was bumped while continuing wide nearing the far turn, made a solid run in the sixth path approaching the stretch but failed to continue. LIQUIDITY angled to the inside in the early stages, settled in good position in the two path along the backstretch, lodged a move along the rail leaving the far turn, angled out slightly while gaining a bit approaching the quarter pole then lacked a further response. BWANA BULL, between horses four or five wide much of the way, never reached contention. STORM IN MAY, outrun near the inside to the stretch, angled out five or six wide but never reached contention. TEUFLESBERG, up close between horses four wide, weakened steadily approaching the stretch. SCAT DADDY raced outside NOBBIZ LIKE SHOWBIZ four or five wide along the backstretch, steadied in tight between horses and was shuffled back nearing the far turn and steadily tired thereafter. STORMELLO attended the early pace under a rating hold five wide, slightly on the backstretch while continuing in contention in the five path, was asked for more three furlongs out, bumped for a stride with CIRCULAR QUAY approaching the stretch and was not persevered with late. COWTOWN CAT, up close between horses early, was finished leaving the backstretch .

YEAR	AGE	STS.	1ST	2ND	3RD	EARNINGS
2006	2	5	2	1	2	$1,178,200
2007	3	8	4	3	0	$3,205,000
TOTALS		13	6	4	2	$4,383,200

At 2 Years WON Breeders' Cup Juvenile; 3RD Breeder's Futurity, Arlington-Washington Breeders' Futurity
At 3 Years WON Kentucky Derby, Travers Stakes, Jim Dandy, Tampa Bay Derby; 2ND Preakness Stakes, Blue Grass Stakes, Kentucky Cup Classic

1875	ARISTIDES	1909	WINTERGREEN	1943	COUNT FLEET	1977	SEATTLE SLEW
1876	VAGRANT	1910	DONAU	1944	PENSIVE	1978	AFFIRMED
1877	BADEN BADEN	1911	MERIDIAN	1945	HOOP JR.	1979	SPECTACULAR BID
1878	DAY STAR	1912	WORTH	1946	ASSAULT	1980	GENUINE RISK
1879	LORD MURPHY	1913	DONERAIL	1947	JET PILOT	1981	PLEASANT COLONY
1880	FONSO	1914	OLD ROSEBUD	1948	CITATION	1982	GATO DEL SOL
1881	HINDOO	1915	REGRET	1949	PONDER	1983	SUNNY'S HALO
1882	APOLLO	1916	GEORGE SMITH	1950	MIDDLEGROUND	1984	SWALE
1883	LEONATUS	1917	OMAR KHAYYAM	1951	COUNT TURF	1985	SPEND A BUCK
1884	BUCHANAN	1918	EXTERMINATOR	1952	HILL GAIL	1986	FERDINAND
1885	JOE COTTON	1919	SIR BARTON	1953	DARK STAR	1987	ALYSHEBA
1886	BEN ALI	1920	PAUL JONES	1954	DETERMINE	1988	WINNING COLORS
1887	MONTROSE	1921	BEHAVE YOURSELF	1955	SWAPS	1989	SUNDAY SILENCE
1888	MACBETH II	1922	MORVICH	1956	NEEDLES	1990	UNBRIDLED
1889	SPOKANE	1923	ZEV	1957	IRON LIEGE	1991	STRIKE THE GOLD
1890	RILEY	1924	BLACK GOLD	1958	TIM TAM	1992	LIL E. TEE
1891	KINGMAN	1925	FLYING EBONY	1959	TOMY LEE	1993	SEA HERO
1892	AZRA	1926	BUBBLING OVER	1960	VENETIAN WAY	1994	GO FOR GIN
1893	LOOKOUT	1927	WHISKERY	1961	CARRY BACK	1995	THUNDER GULCH
1894	CHANT	1928	REIGH COUNT	1962	DECIDEDLY	1996	GRINDSTONE
1895	HALMA	1929	CLYDE VAN DUSEN	1963	CHATEAUGAY	1997	SILVER CHARM
1896	BEN BRUSH	1930	GALLANT FOX	1964	NORTHERN DANCER	1998	REAL QUIET
1897	TYPHOON II	1931	TWENTY GRAND	1965	LUCKY DEBONAIR	1999	CHARISMATIC
1898	PLAUDIT	1932	BURGOO KING	1966	KAUAI KING	2000	FUSAICHI PEGASUS
1899	MANUEL	1933	BROKERS TIP	1967	PROUD CLARION	2001	MONARCHOS
1900	LIEUT. GIBSON	1934	CAVALCADE	1968	FORWARD PASS	2002	WAR EMBLEM
1901	HIS EMINENCE	1935	OMAHA	1969	MAJESTIC PRINCE	2003	FUNNY CIDE
1902	ALAN-A-DALE	1936	BOLD VENTURE	1970	DUST COMMANDER	2004	SMARTY JONES
1903	JUDGE HIMES	1937	WAR ADMIRAL	1971	CANONERO II	2005	GIACOMO
1904	ELWOOD	1938	LAWRIN	1972	RIVA RIDGE	2006	BARBARO
1905	AGILE	1939	JOHNSTOWN	1973	SECRETARIAT	2007	STREET SENSE
1906	SIR HUON	1940	GALLAHADION	1974	CANNONADE		
1907	PINK STAR	1941	WHIRLAWAY	1975	FOOLISH PLEASURE		
1908	STONE STREET	1942	SHUT OUT	1976	BOLD FORBES